Flavo[

Croatia

Discover the Flavors of Croatia With
the Help of These Recipes!

BY: Allie Allen

COOK & ENJOY

Copyright 2020 Allie Allen

Copyright Notes

This book is written as an informational tool. While the author has taken every precaution to ensure the accuracy of the information provided therein, the reader is warned that they assume all risk when following the content. The author will not be held responsible for any damages that may occur as a result of the readers' actions.

The author does not give permission to reproduce this book in any form, including but not limited to: print, social media posts, electronic copies or photocopies, unless permission is expressly given in writing.

Table of Contents

Introduction

Looking to explore the wonderful flavors of Croatia? If so, this cookbook is for you! Filled with the most delicious and mouth-watering recipes, this cookbook will teach you how to whip up delicious, flavorful dishes straight from Croatia! Using simple ingredients, you'll be able to put up beautiful dishes that'll impress your friends and family!

With the help of just one cookbook, you'll get a taste of Croatia recipes that come with simple instructions and can be easily doubled or tripled. So what are you waiting for? Let's get cooking!

1. Squid Stew

This dish will give you a look at Croatian cooking on your table at home. This special stew is one of many inspired by the proximity of Croatia to the Mediterranean coast.

Makes: 2-4 Servings

Prep: 10 mins

Cook: 50 mins

Ingredients:

- 4 minced cloves of garlic
- 2 minced onions, medium
- Several leaves of celery
- 17 1/2 oz. of chick peas
- 21 oz. of squid, cut into small pieces
- Olive oil
- Shrimp broth
- Rocket salad
- Parsley

Directions:

Heat oil in large roasting pan. Add garlic and onion several leaves of celery. Once these ingredients have softened, add tiny pieces of squid meat. As it softens, add the shrimp broth. This will give it extra flavor. Add chick peas. Boil stew for 45-50 minutes.

Place rocket salad on individual plates. Cover with stew. You may add other ingredients from the sea, too, like octopus or ink fish. Serve.

2. Croatian Sauerkraut

Although well known in Germany, sauerkraut is a traditional dish in Croatia as well.

Makes: 12 Servings

Prep: 10 mins

Cook: 1 hr. 20 mins

Ingredients:

- 1/2 cup of water, purified
- 1/2 pound of bacon
- 3 minced garlic cloves
- Cooking spray
- 1 x 32-ounce jar sauerkraut
- 3 chopped onions
- 1 x 8-oz. can tomato sauce
- 2 tbsp. of bouillon, vegetable
- Ground pepper, as desired

Directions:

Heat oven to 375F.

Rinse the sauerkraut using cold water. Set it aside.

Cover baking sheet with aluminum foil. Place bacon on this sheet. Cook for 12 to 15 minutes.

Spray large pot with non-stick spray on med. heat. Add garlic onion and cook for four-five minutes, until they are browning slightly and becoming translucent.

Add the sauerkraut. Sprinkle bouillon and mix them. Add water and tomato sauce. Remove bacon from oven. Add 1 tbsp. bacon fat to pot. Chop bacon into small pieces. Mix with sauerkraut.

Cover pot. Slowly steam for an hour on low heat, stirring occasionally. Serve in individual bowls.

3. Radish Salad

This dish uses fresh radishes; they are red outside but white inside. The recipe is refreshing and crisp.

Makes: 4 Servings

Prep: 20 mins

Cook: -

Ingredients:

- 2 trimmed, sliced bunches of radishes, small
- 1 tbsp. of parsley, minced
- 2 tbsp. of oil, olive
- 1 tsp. of thyme, minced
- 2 tbsp. of mayonnaise
- Salt, kosher, as desired
- Ground pepper, black, as desired

Directions:

Whisk the mayo, salt, pepper, thyme, parsley and oil in medium sized bowl. Add radishes and stir.

Chill the sauerkraut for about 15 minutes. Serve.

4. Brussels Sprouts Casserole

A delicious casserole with Brussel sprouts and bread crumbs.

Makes: 1-2 Servings

Prep: 10 mins

Cook: 25 mins

Ingredients:

- 1 egg, large
- 6 3/4 oz. of sour cream
- 7 oz. of fresh cottage cheese
- 14 oz. of Brussels sprouts
- Oil
- Bread crumbs
- Kosher salt ground black pepper

Directions:

Clean the Brussels sprouts well. Slice.

Put Brussels sprouts in boiling water, pre-salted. Before they become soft, drain.

Mix salt, pepper, sour cream and cottage cheese.

Mix that with Brussels sprouts. Pour all into baking dish.

Sprinkle top using bread crumbs and drizzle with a bit of oil.

Bake in oven at 350F until casserole is golden brown. Serve.

5. Croatian Pepper Tomato Stew

This dish is delicious and quick, and you can make it year-round.

Makes: 5 Servings

Prep: 10 mins

Cook: 15 mins

Ingredients:

- Olive oil
- 1 julienned onion
- 3 yellow or Hungarian wax bananas
- 3 chopped, medium tomatoes
- Salt, sea

Directions:

Caramelize onions on medium pot on med. heat.

Add a bit of salt and peppers. Cook until they are starting to become soft.

Add tomatoes and 1/2 tsp. of sea salt.

Cook for five to eight minutes. Stir occasionally as tomatoes are releasing their juice and cooking into stew.

Taste and season as desired. Serve.

6. Risotto with Cuttlefish

This risotto is less like Italian food and more a stew with rice that features seafood as a main ingredient. The flavor is different than many other risotto dishes, and it's quite incredible.

Makes: 6-8 Servings

Prep: 10 mins

Cook: 30 mins

Ingredients:

- 3 tbsp. of parsley, minced
- 1/4 cup of white wine, dry
- 1 cup of rice, Arborio
- 6 tbsp. of oil, olive
- 3 pounds of cuttlefish, raw, cleaned, sliced, ink reserved
- 6 cups of fish stock
- 4 minced garlic cloves
- 5 minced shallots, medium
- 1 tbsp. of lemon juice
- 1 tsp. of lemon zest, grated
- Salt, kosher, as desired
- Ground pepper, as desired

Directions:

Heat the stock in small sauce pan on med. heat and keep warm.

Heat 1/2 oil in large sauce pan on med-high.

Add half of garlic and half of shallots. Cook for three to four minutes, until they are soft.

Add cuttlefish and cook, occasionally stirring, until they are tender.

Transfer to bowl. Cover. Set the bowl aside.

Add the rest of the oil to a pan. Heat on med-high. Cook the rest of the garlic and shallots till they are soft. Add the rice cook until it has toasted lightly.

Add wine and stir. Cook until it evaporates.

Add 1/2 cup of heated stock. Stir while cooking until it is absorbed.

Continue to add stock and cook until it is absorbed.

Add more rice until mixture is creamy and tender. Add ink and stir until rice has been coated and is black in color.

Remove pot from heat. Add parsley, lemon juice and zest, and finally salt and ground pepper. Serve in individual bowls.

7. Pork Cracklings

This is a typical kind of snack in Croatia and is most popular in the Northern regions of Croatia.

Makes: 12 Servings

Prep: 10 mins

Cook: 20 mins

Ingredients:

- 1 3/4 ounces of milk, whole
- 6 pounds of pig bacon, white, raw
- Salt, coarse

Directions:

Pick raw bacon from back of pork. Use knife to remove skin and cut into cubes of about an inch each.

Place bacon cubes in deep-fry pot over med. heat. Once bacon has released fat, stir with large spoon.

Allow cubes of cracklings to sizzle in the fat. Continue stirring until they are brownish.

Add milk to cracklings. This provides crispness and color.

After fat has cleared, remove the cracklings from pot. Drain them well.

Salt as desired and serve.

8. Sardine Brodetto

You will commonly hear in the country of Croatia that the region of Dalmatia has been fed with sardines for many years. These small fish are found abundantly in the Adriatic Sea, and are used in various dishes in Croatia, including this recipe.

Makes: 3 Servings

Prep: 10 mins

Cook: 15 mins

Ingredients:

- 4 tomatoes, medium
- 15 fillets, sardine
- 3 garlic cloves
- 1 medium onion, yellow
- Laurel leaf
- 6 3/4 ounces of wine
- Small rosemary branch
- 3 sage plant leaves
- Corn grits
- Olive oil
- Basil leaves

Directions:

Cover fillets in flour on both sides. Fry in oil. Place them on paper towels to release the excess oil.

In a pan, fry onions in olive oil until they are golden in color. Add minced garlic for just a second or two. Add herbs and tomatoes. Once sauce has thickened, add wine.

Add sardines. Taste and adjust seasonings, as desired.

Prepare the corn grits by cooking in water. Serve next to the sardine brodetto.

9. Potatoes Chard

This traditional dish is quite easy to pull together. It works as a side dish for cured meats, fish and cooked meats.

Makes: 4-6 Servings

Prep: 10 mins

Cook: 15 mins

Ingredients:

- 6 sliced garlic cloves
- 1 pound of peeled, cubed potatoes
- 1 pound of Swiss chard with tougher stems removed and more tender stems + leaves torn roughly into 2-inch pieces
- 1/3 cup of oil, olive
- Salt, coarse
- Pepper, ground, black

Directions:

Boil the potatoes in medium sauce pan with salted water till barely tender, about five to seven minutes. Drain potatoes and set them aside.

Add oil to the pan. Heat on med-high. Add the garlic and cook till it is soft. Add the potatoes. Stir occasionally while cooking, until they are golden – usually five to seven minutes.

Stir in the Swiss chard. Cook for five minutes or so, until it is wilted. Season using coarse salt and ground pepper, as desired. Serve.

10. Pumpkin Soup

Pumpkin soup does not change a great deal from one country to the next, and it's made all over the world.

Makes: 3-4 Servings

Prep: 15 mins

Cook: 20 mins

Ingredients:

- 2 cups of milk, whole
- 3/4 cup of potatoes, diced
- 5 cups of pumpkin, peeled, diced
- 1 tbsp. of butter, unsalted
- 1/2 cup of onion, diced
- 1 stock cube, chicken
- 2 cups of water, filtered
- A pinch of nutmeg, ground
- A pinch of ginger, ground
- Kosher salt ground pepper, as desired

Directions:

Cook the onions in unsalted butter in large sized sauce pan.

Add nutmeg, ginger, water, potatoes and pumpkin. Use kosher salt and ground pepper to season.

Cook for about 18-20 minutes. Potatoes and pumpkin should be tender.

Add the milk. Blend till consistency is smooth. Serve.

11. Pasta Fazol

This thick stew with pasta and beans works especially well in cold weather, when you want a dish to warm you up.

Makes: 4-6 Servings

Prep: 10 mins

Cook: 35 mins

Ingredients:

- 1 quart of broth, vegetable
- 3 1/2 oz. of pancetta (cured bacon from pork belly)
- 10 1/2 oz. of beans, canned or cooked
- 1 onion, medium
- 1 carrot
- 2 garlic cloves
- 5 1/3 oz. of pasta (your favorite type)
- Olive oil for frying
- 2 laurel leaves
- Celery
- Parsley
- Thyme

Directions:

Mince carrot, celery, garlic and onion. Fry in olive oil. Add broth till they have softened.

Chop the pancetta into small sized pieces. Add to pan. Add broth as needed.

In another pan, cook beans. Add beans to mixture in original pan. Add salt, pepper, parsley, thyme and laurel.

Cook for 1/2 hour over med. heat.

In separate pan, cook the pasta until it is al dente. Add to mixture. Stir to combine and serve.

12. Pod Peku (Baby Goat Veal)

This dish traces its history back over 500 years in the region now known as Croatia. It is often served during religious holidays or feast days.

Makes: 4 Servings

Prep: 15 mins

Cook: 2 hrs. 15 mins

Ingredients:

- 1/2 cup of oil, olive
- 1 3/4 pounds of meat, goat
- 2 3/4 pounds of veal (from neck or thigh)
- 1/2 pound of potatoes, medium
- 1/3 ounce of peppercorns, black
- 1/3 ounce of rosemary
- 1/5 ounce of lard
- 1/3 lb. of spring onions
- 1 bay leaf
- Salt, coarse

Directions:

Spread lard into bottom of large-sized pot.

Cut meat into several pieces if it seems large. Salt and place in pot.

Peel the potato. Cut into pieces. Salt place under meat.

Place peppercorns, rosemary, bay leaf and onion into pot. Pour in olive oil. Cover pan with foil. Bake at 390F for 1 1/2 hours.

Uncover and check meat for doneness. Cut large pieces in smaller ones. Bake mixture for 1/2 hour to 45 minutes more. Serve in individual bowls.

13. Sauerkraut Salted Pork

This dish will transport you in mind to the beautiful country of Croatia. It is sometimes served with boiled potatoes.

Makes: 2-3 Servings

Prep: 10 mins

Cook: 40 mins

Ingredients:

- 5 tbsp. of sour cream
- 21 ounces of sauerkraut
- 15 ounces of beans, soaked the night before using
- 1 pound of diced potatoes
- 1 pound of salt pork
- 1/2 cup of fat
- Water, as needed
- 1 chopped onion, medium
- 1 heaping tbsp. of flour, all-purpose
- Salt, coarse, as desired
- Peppercorns, as desired
- 3 cloves of garlic
- 3 bay leaves

Directions:

Heat thin layer of fat oil in casserole dish. Brown meat fully.

Add onion and sauerkraut. Allow to cook till they are transparent.

Add beans and potatoes. Stir as they start cooking.

Add flour and rest of fat or oil. Stir fully until flour covers all ingredients and is mixing with juices.

Cover with stock. Cook for 35-40 minutes. Meat should be tender and veggies should be cooked through. Add sour cream and serve.

14. Oil Vinegar Potato Salad

This potato salad recipe is different from dishes by the same name served elsewhere. There is no sour cream or mayonnaise used for binding the veggies and potatoes, so it's a more versatile and long-lasting food for picnics and get-togethers.

Makes: 6 Servings

Prep: 10 mins plus overnight

Cook: -

Ingredients:

- 2 halved, sliced yellow onions, medium
- 6 boiled, peeled, sliced potatoes, large, Yukon Gold or white
- 1/2 cup of oil, olive
- 1/4 cup of vinegar, white
- 1 chopped red pepper, roasted
- 1 chopped garlic clove
- 2 tbsp. of sugar, granulated
- 1 1/2 tsp. of salt, coarse
- 1/2 tsp. of pepper, black

Directions:

Place onions and potatoes in large sized bowl.

Add black pepper, sugar, salt, red pepper, garlic, oil and vinegar to a jar with a screw top.

Cover with lid. Vigorously shake. Toss the potatoes with the dressing.

Cover and refrigerate overnight.

Allow to sit till it hits room temperature for best flavor.

Taste. Adjust any seasonings you desire. Serve.

15. Croatian Mussels

Cooking mussels or other shellfish in olive oil and garlic is a traditional way to prepare them in Croatia.

Makes: 4 Servings

Prep: 10 mins

Cook: 10 mins

Ingredients:

- 8 chopped cloves of garlic
- 4 lbs. of mussels
- 3/4 cup bread crumbs, fresh
- 1 1/4 cups of white wine, dry
- 1/4 cup of chopped parsley, fresh
- 3/4 cup of oil, olive
- A dash of sea salt
- A dash of pepper, black

Directions:

Scrub and then de-beard the mussels.

Add the mussels, along with garlic, parsley and olive oil to large-sized, heated skillet.

Allow this mixture to simmer without disturbing it, till mussels are just starting to open.

While stirring, lower the heat. Add the white wine, salt and pepper as desired. Do not over-salt. Mussels are salty already.

Allow all mussel shells to open, while still stirring occasionally. If any shells don't open, discard those mussels.

Raise heat once more to finish cooking without making the mussel meat tough.

Mix bread crumbs in broth. Leave some of the liquid present.

Serve with nice thick crusty bread to help you soak up broth.

16. Little Čvarkuše Treats

Čvarkuše are flaky, salt, rich pastries served as snacks traditionally, in many areas of Croatia.

Makes: 4 Servings

Prep: 45 mins

Cook: 20 mins

Ingredients:

- 1 egg, large
- 2 3/4 oz. of sifted flour, all-purpose
- 1 beaten egg yolk + 1 tbsp. water to make egg wash
- 1 tbsp. of cubed butter, cold
- 1 to 2 tbsp. of wine, white
- 1 tsp. of sugar, granulated
- 1 cube of yeast, fresh
- 1 1/2 ounces of pork cracklings
- 6 3/4 fl. oz. of milk, whole

Directions:

Preheat your oven to 395F.

Crush yeast into sugar and milk. Allow to rise.

Sift flour into large sized bowl. Create a divot (hole) in middle of flour. Add the salt. Place yeast mixture in divot, as well.

Knead well till all ingredients are incorporated. You can use more milk if you need to.

Add egg, wine, cracklings and lard.

Knead until dough has become soft and elastic. Cover with damp towel. Allow to rest for 1/2 hour.

Knead three more times with 1/2-hour resting intervals between.

Roll dough out. Use round cookie cutter to press circles out.

Arrange these Čvarkuše in baking tray. Brush top with beaten egg yolk.

Bake in 395F oven for 18-20 minutes. Čvarkuše should turn golden brown. Serve.

17. Potato Tuna Moussaka

This moussaka recipe shows the culinary influence of Turkish and Greek cuisine in Croatia. This one is not made with eggplant, though. The potatoes make an excellent substitute. In addition, this dish uses an egg custard on top, instead of the white sauce more commonly used in Greece.

Makes: 3-4 Servings

Prep: 10 mins

Cook: 20 mins

Ingredients:

- 1 3/4 oz. of grated cheese
- 1 tbsp. pf parsley, chopped
- 10 fl. oz. sour cream
- 17 1/2 oz. of smooth or salad potatoes, scrubbed and thinly sliced
- 7-oz. of rinsed, drained sweetcorn
- 1 x 14-oz. can of drained tuna packaged in brine

Directions:

Place potatoes in a pot of boiling slightly salted water.

Cover. Simmer for 8-10 minutes, until potatoes are tender.

Drain. Allow potatoes to cool down a bit.

Mix tuna with parsley, sour cream and sweet corn. Cook on med. heat for three to four minutes.

Place 1/2 potatoes on base of oven-proof casserole dish.

Pour tuna mixture over the potatoes.

Place the rest of the potatoes over the top of the tuna mixture.

Sprinkle with cheese. Place casserole dish under hot grill for two to three minutes. Top should be golden brown. Serve alongside a salad.

18. Croatian Bean Soup

This soup recipe ends up so delectably thick that it could be called a stew. The name literally translates to "beans and stew". You can use it as a main dish for lunch or dinner, but it is more often used as an appetizer before a hearty main course.

Makes: 8 Servings

Prep: 10 mins plus overnight

Cook: 2-3 hrs.

Ingredients:

- 12-15 cups of filtered water, cold
- 1 lb. of beans, dried, rinsed, picked over, soaked
- 1 large chopped onion
- 3 peeled, minced garlic cloves
- 1 lb. of smoke sausage, cut in 4" lengths
- 1 bay leaf, large
- 1 lb. of ribs, smoked
- Sea salt, ground pepper seasoning, as desired

Directions:

Place rinsed and picked through beans in large sized pot. Add water to a level about three inches over beans. Cover. Soak overnight without refrigerating.

The next day, when preparing to cook this dish, drain beans. Rinse and re-drain. Place in large sized pot. Add 12 cups of cold, fresh water.

Bring to boil reduce heat to simmer. Skim off foam if any rises to surface.

Add Vegeta seasoning, salt, pepper, bay leaf, smoked ribs, smoked sausage, onion and garlic.

Return mixture to boil. Lower heat and allow stew to simmer, covered partially, for two or three hours. Meat and beans should be tender. Add water if needed and stir occasionally.

Remove and discard bay leaf. Remove the bones from rib meat. Return meat only to pot.

Serve in large bowls with a hearty bread.

19. Shopska Salad

In addition to being prepared often in Croatia, this salad is known in Romania, Serbia and Macedonia. It brings together onion, cucumbers, peppers and tomatoes in a dish that sparkles with olive oil.

Makes: 2-4 Servings

Prep: 10 mins

Cook: 10 mins

Ingredients:

- 1 cucumber
- 3 or 4 tomatoes
- 1 onion, medium
- 5 1/3 oz. of sheep's cheese, brined
- 4 to 5 peppers
- Oil, olive
- Vinegar
- Parsley
- Salt, coarse

Directions:

Dice the veggies. Bake, then peel and remove seeds from peppers. Cut them into thin strips. Add onion, diced tomatoes and cucumbers.

Add vinegar, salt and oil. Mix and combine.

Top using grated cheese and chopped parsley. Serve.

20. Apricots Spiced Lamb

Apricots in a main dish? Yes! You may not have cooked with apricots before, but they present a wonderful addition to this dish.

Makes: 6-8 Servings

Prep: 2 hrs.

Cook: 15 mins

Ingredients:

- 1 onion, red, cut in 8ths
- 5 1/2 pounds of lamb loin, boneless, trimmed, cubed
- Boiling water
- 24 apricots, dried
- 1/4 cup of vinegar, red wine
- 2 tbsp. of chopped shallots
- 1/2 cup of jam, apricot
- 2 tbsp. of oil, olive
- 1 tbsp. of sugar, dark brown
- 1 tsp. of mustard, dry
- 2 tbsp. of water, filtered
- 1 tsp. of coriander, ground
- 1 tsp. of lemon juice, fresh
- Salt, coarse
- Pepper, ground

Directions:

In small sized bowl, plump the 24 apricots in boiling water. Drain.

In a larger bowl, combine red wine vinegar, apricot jam, plus 2 tbsp. each of filtered water, shallots and olive oil.

Stir in the brown sugar, along with 1 tsp. each of lemon juice, coriander and mustard.

Add the boneless, trimmed lamb loin cubes. Toss and combine. Cover. Refrigerate for two hours.

Preheat the grill to med-high heat.

Thread the 8ths of onion, along with lamb and apricots onto 8 x 12" skewers. Season as desired using salt ground pepper.

Cover. Grill on well-oiled grate for seven to nine minutes if you prefer med-rare. Turn once. Serve.

21. Soparnik

Soparnik is sometimes called Croatian pizza, but it's actually more similar to pie, since it has dough both on bottom and on top. It is often made with Swiss chard but is sometimes made with kale.

Makes: 4 Servings

Prep: 20 mins

Cook: 20 mins

Ingredients:

- 1 spring onion
- 2 1/4 pounds of Swiss chard
- 3 tbsp. of oil, olive
- 4 cups of flour, all-purpose
- 1 bunch of parsley
- 4 cloves
- 1 cup of filtered water
- Salt, coarse

Directions:

Wash chard. Cut out stalks. Cut chard into thin strips. Place in medium bowl.

Chop parsley and spring onion. Add to bowl with chard.

Add salt as desired. Sprinkle using olive oil.

Sift flour in large bowl. Add water, 3 tbsp. oil and salt. Mix together with a hand mixer add water as you need it, until the mixture binds.

Sprinkle flour on baking tray. Place round pastry shape on it. Add chard mixture. Cover with other 1/2 of pastry, also rolled into round shape.

Tuck in pastry edges to enclose the shapes.

Place in oven at 390F for 18-20 minutes.

Crush the garlic into small amount of olive oil. Use it to paste top of cooked Soparnik. Slice. Serve.

22. Saffron Shrimp

This is a wonderful combination of seafood, beans, pasta and veggies. It also goes from prep to plate in less than an hour.

Makes: 2-4 Servings

Prep: 20 mins

Cook: 10 mins

Ingredients:

- 8 shrimps, large
- 12 oz. of barley, pearl
- 6 oz. teacup broad beans, boiled
- 1 tomato, medium
- 2 spoons of chopped parsley
- 2 chopped onions, fresh
- 2 oz. of oil, olive
- 3/4 oz. of saffron
- Oil, sunflower
- 1 lemon, juice and zest only
- Sea salt
- Ground pepper

Directions:

Boil pearl barley in pre-salted water. Strain. Rinse using cold water. Sprinkle a bit of sunflower oil to keep it from sticking.

Soak the saffron in 2 spoon-fuls of lukewarm water. Set aside for 15 minutes.

When saffron has released its aroma and color, mix in lemon zest and juice, olive oil and then sprinkle using sea salt ground pepper.

Clean shrimps and salt them.

Sauté shrimps for several moments in a bit of olive oil on strong heat.

Cut tomato in 1/2. Remove the seeds. Slice thinly.

Mix barley with shrimps, parsley, onions, tomato and broad beans.

Add dressing. Serve.

23. Zagorje Soup

Zagorje is the region that this soup comes from, in the northern area of Croatia. The small towns and villages in the hillsides of the area are well-suited to agriculture, as exemplified by the ingredients in this tasty soup.

Makes: 3-4 Servings

Prep: 10 mins

Cook: 15 mins

Ingredients:

- 10 1/2 oz. of mushrooms, Portobello
- 1 onion, medium, chopped
- 2 sausages
- 4 potatoes, medium
- 6 3/4 fl. oz. of sour cream
- 2 tbsp. of vinegar
- 2 cloves of garlic, chopped
- Oil
- Parsley
- Salt, kosher
- Pepper, black, ground

Directions:

Fry chopped garlic and onion in the oil. Then stir in mushrooms. Allow to sear until the liquid has evaporated.

Add the sliced sausage and fry gently. Add in potato cubes. Pour in water as needed so that potatoes are covered.

Mix salt, pepper, flour and sour cream. Drizzle into the soup.

Leave mixture to simmer till the potatoes have softened.

Add parsley and vinegar. Cook for a few more minutes. Serve.

24. Chicken Paprikas

This meal comes from the northwest corner of Croatia. It's quite popular along the river Drava.

Makes: 4 Servings

Prep: 15 mins

Cook: 50 mins

Ingredients:

- 2 minced onions, large
- 2 1/4 pounds of chicken pieces, breasts or back pieces with skin and bones
- 3 tsp. of paprika, ground
- 2/10 pound of lard
- 1/2 tsp. of salt, coarse
- 1/4 tsp. of chili
- 1/2 tsp. of caraway seeds
- 1 1/3 cups of water, filtered
- 1 tsp. of pepper, black
- 1/10 pound of sour cream
- 1 7/8 cup of wine, white

Directions:

Melt lard in large-sized pot.

Add minced onions. Sauté until onions are transparent and soft.

Chop chicken into little pieces. Add them to pot. Sauté till meat turns white.

Add the wine. Sauté for about five additional minutes.

Add 3 tsp. of paprika and chili as desired, plus caraway seeds, coarse salt and ground pepper.

Add water sufficient that chicken is covered.

Sauté for 45-50 minutes. Chicken should be soft.

Add two to three tsp. of sour cream. Cook for three to five additional minutes.

Serve alone or with mashed potatoes or noodles, your preference.

25. Cevapcici

These are tasty little kebabs and are generally made with beef. As in other Mediterranean countries, it is usually served with a dip that includes roasted red peppers.

Makes: 6-8 Servings

Prep: 10 mins

Cook: 15 mins

Ingredients:

- 18 ounces of beef, minced
- 1 chopped onion, large
- 1 minced garlic clove
- 1 large egg, white only
- 1 tsp. of salt, sea
- 1 tsp. of ground pepper
- 1/2 tsp. of paprika

Directions:

Combine all ingredients in large-sized bowl. Work with your fingers till meat is mixed well with all of the other ingredients. This usually takes 10-15 minutes.

Take small hand-ful of mixture for each of the Cevapcici you are making. Roll into a fat kebab, with the shape of a sausage.

Cover in plastic wrap. Place in refrigerator for one hour. This will help the ingredients to bond together. They can also be put into freezer at this time, until you're ready to use them.

Cook Cevapcici in broiler of your oven until they cook through. You can cook them over a charcoal grill, if you prefer. They must be cooked well done.

Serve with onions, bread or white cheese.

26. Healthy Nut Cake

You don't often hear "healthy" and "cake" in the same recipe. This cake brings taste to the table without using cream fat, flour or eggs. Instead, you will use oils and foods with healthy omega fatty acids.

Makes: 3-4 Servings

Prep: 3-4 hrs.

Cook: -

Ingredients:

- 3 cups of cashews
- 2 cups of almonds
- 3/4 cup of maple syrup + 1/2 cup for the top layer
- 3 tbsp. of powdered chocolate or carob
- 1/2 cup of milk, almond
- 1 1/4 cups of coconut oil + 1 for the top layer
- 1 vanilla bean
- 1 pinch sea salt, coarse

Directions:

Add 3 tbsp. coconut oil, 3 tbsp. syrup, plus carob and almonds in food processor. Mix at high speed.

Process till almonds have been fully chopped and have released their oils.

In circle-shaped baking pan, pour mixture in evenly. Allow to cool in refrigerator. This is bottom layer of the cake.

Clean out pitcher of food processor. Add cashews, salt, almond milk, 1 cup of coconut oil and 1/2 cup of syrup.

Cut vanilla pod open. Scrape seeds into food processor.

Process till cashews are chopped and nuts have released their oils.

Remove first cake layer from fridge. Spread cashew paste atop almond layer. Smooth cashew layer with spatula. Place cake in freezer. Freeze for several hours, at least.

Allow to thaw as needed. Serve.

27. Croatian Blackberry Pie

This blackberry pastry is just as flaky and buttery as you would think. The filling is fluffy and light, and the berries balance the pie's sweetness. You won't have any leftovers.

Makes: 6 Servings

Prep: 15 mins

Cook: 50 mins

Ingredients:

- 1 lb. of blackberries
- 2 separated eggs, large
- 3/4 tsp. of baking powder
- 1 cup of flour, plain
- 1 cup of sugar, granulated
- 6 oz. of butter, cold, unsalted
- 1 tsp. of lemon zest
- 1 tsp. of vanilla extract, pure
- For serving: confectioner's sugar

Directions:

Process 1/2 cup of granulated sugar, butter, baking powder and flour in the food processor until the mixture looks like bread crumbs.

Add 2 egg yolks. Process till mixture has formed a ball. The dough should be soft. Turn out on to a cutting board with flour on it.

Reserve 1/3 of dough. Shape into a circle. Cover with cling wrap. Refrigerate for 1/2 hour.

Dampen your hands and use them to press the rest of the dough into the sides and base of a lined, greased 8-inch pie dish. Place the pie shell in refrigerator for chilling.

Preheat the oven at 350 degrees F.

To create the filling, use electric mixer to whisk the egg whites into soft peaks. Add last 1/2 cup of sugar. Whisk until glossy and thick.

Fold in lemon zest, blackberries and vanilla until they are combined well. Spoon the mixture into the pastry shell.

Slice off little pieces of the reserved dough. Place over the filling and cover.

Bake for 45-50 minutes, till pastry is golden in color. Serve cold or warm, dusted with confectioner's sugar.

28. Chestnut Cocoa Dessert

This is a unique dish, with tastes that are not combined that often. The chestnuts offer a rich, sweet, starchy flavor that complements the cocoa.

Makes: 3-5 Servings

Prep: 15 mins

Cook: 30 mins

Ingredients:

For the cups:

- 2 spoons full of breadcrumbs
- 1 3/4 ounces of butter, unsalted
- 3 ounces of butter, softened
- 3 eggs, large
- 1 3/4 oz. of sugar, muscovado (molasses-infused sugar)
- 3 1/2 oz. of crystal sugar
- 1 spoon of cocoa
- 4 1/4 oz. of flour, chestnut
- 3 1/2 ounces of cranberries, dried
- 3 1/3 fl. oz. of milk, whole
- 1 spoon of baking powder

Directions:

Heat oven to 350F. Prepare baking cups. Smear with crumbs and butter.

Remove yolks from whites of eggs. Mix whites till they have a texture like snow.

In a separate bowl, combine the yolks with both types of sugar. Add milk and butter.

After mixing well, add baking powder, chestnut flour and cocoa.

Replace mixer arm of mixer with ladle. Gently stir. Put egg white mixture and the cranberries in bowl.

Insert mixture into baking cups. Leave in oven for about 1/2 hour. Serve hot.

29. Walnut Sˇtrukli

There are a few variations of this dessert, and if you travel to Croatia, be sure to try it in several locations, if you can. It is a bit labor-intensive for a home dessert, but worth it.

Makes: 4 Servings

Prep: 15 mins

Cook: 45 mins

Ingredients:

- 1 1/4 cups of cream
- 6 3/4 tbsp. of sour cream
- 1 3/8 cups of cottage cheese
- 2 3/8 cups of walnuts
- 2 3/4 cups of flour, all-purpose
- 7 1/8 tbsp. of raisins
- 5/8 cup of milk, whole
- 2 eggs, large
- 1 tsp. of vanilla sugar
- 4 tbsp. of sugar, granulated
- 1 tbsp. of honey, pure
- 1 tsp. of cinnamon, ground
- 2 tbsp. of oil, olive
- 7 tbsp. of butter, unsalted
- A pinch of salt, coarse

Directions:

To create dough, mix water, salt, oil, egg and flour. Once it is combined into a dough, then drizzle with oil to avoid drying out. Set aside for 1/2 hour.

Pour milk into heated pan. Add walnuts, honey, cinnamon, raisins and 2 tbsp. of sugar. Cook for a bit and set aside so it can cool.

In another bowl, mix vanilla sugar, granulated sugar, sour cream, an egg and cottage cheese. Add to cooled walnut/milk mixture.

Stretch dough out on flour-sprinkled cloth. It should be thin, but not at risk of breaking.

Add mixture onto first row of dough in 4-inch lots. Roll cloth away from you. After rolling, cut dough into Štrukli shapes (like little burritos). Place in dish with melted butter.

Pour the cream over the top. Bake for 45 minutes at 390F. Sprinkle with cinnamon and icing sugar. Serve.

30. Jam Crescent Cookies

This is a classic kifle cookie that is quite popular all over Croatia. It was once baked mainly during the holiday season, but now they are made throughout the year. You can stuff these cookies with your favorite jam.

Makes: 12 Servings

Prep: 15 mins

Cook: 15 mins

Ingredients:

- 1 1/2 tsp. of baking powder
- 3 2/3 cups of flour, pastry
- 2/3 cup of sour cream
- 2 sticks of butter, unsalted
- 1/2 tsp. of lemon zest, fresh
- 1 tbsp. of sugar, confectioners
- 1 1/2 cups of jam – plum or apricot
- A pinch of sea salt, coarse
- To dust: confectioner's sugar

Directions:

In food processor, mix butter with baking powder, salt, lemon zest, confectioner's sugar and sour cream. Don't overmix. Wrap dough in cling wrap. Chill in your refrigerator for eight hours (overnight is fine) or freeze for an hour or so.

Roll 1/4 of dough into thin circle on floured cutting board. Cut circle into six triangles.

Put 1/2 tsp. of jam on each triangle. Jam must be firm, not runny.

Roll the triangles into crescent shapes.

Arrange cookies on baking sheet. Bake in 350-degree F oven for 15 minutes. Their color should remain pale.

Transfer cookies to wire rack for cooling. Dust with confectioner's sugar. Serve.

Conclusion

Well, there you go folks! 30 delicious recipes straight from the heart of Croatia! Make sure you try out all these wonderful delicacies and don't forget to share with your friends and family!

About the Author

Allie Allen developed her passion for the culinary arts at the tender age of five when she would help her mother cook for their large family of 8. Even back then, her family knew this would be more than a hobby for the young Allie and when she graduated from high school, she applied to cooking school in London. It had always been a dream of the young chef to study with some of Europe's best and she made it happen by attending the Chef Academy of London.

After graduation, Allie decided to bring her skills back to North America and open up her own restaurant. After 10 successful years as head chef and owner, she decided to sell her business and pursue other career avenues. This monumental decision led Allie to her true calling, teaching. She also started to write e-books for her students to study at home for practice. She is now the proud author of several e-books and gives private and semi-private cooking lessons to a range of students at all levels of experience.

Stay tuned for more from this dynamic chef and teacher when she releases more informative e-books on cooking and baking in the near future. Her work is infused with stores and anecdotes you will love!

Author's Afterthoughts

I can't tell you how grateful I am that you decided to read my book. My most heartfelt thanks that you took time out of your life to choose my work and I hope you find benefit within these pages.

There are so many books available today that offer similar content so that makes it even more humbling that you decided to buying mine.

Tell me what you thought! I am eager to hear your opinion and ideas on what you read as are others who are looking for a good book to buy. Leave a review on Amazon.com so others can benefit from your wisdom!

With much thanks,

Allie Allen

Printed in Great Britain
by Amazon

12722428R00058